The Death Transition

by

Cliff Aguirre

Second Edition

Published by Williams & Gold Communication

Williamsgoldcom@yahoo.com

A Kindle version can be found at Amazon.com

Table of Contents

Communicating with Loved Ones
in Spirit

Reminders

As the curtain falls and the lights grow dim this show becomes nothingness in the eyes of the audience. But we shall continue on, to a new stage, act a new play, and receive the applause of yet another audience. The old audience sees death, the new audience sees birth; I gain a new life. Someday we will meet on that distant stage and you will understand that there is no beginning and no end.

- Cliff Aguirre -

Foreword

The Death Transition was written with the intention of presenting a positive understanding of death, in order to quell the fear of death, which seems to be the common reaction to dying.

My purpose is to try to answer many of the questions surrounding the mystery of death and to go beyond the speculation of other books that deal with death and dying and provide a proven roadmap for our ongoing existence.

In writing this book, help was given in communicating the information by individuals who would be considered "dead" personalities. Their desire was to convey to the readers the process and experience of death through first-hand knowledge.

I have learned through the years to communicate with these "dead" personalities by allowing myself to share in their continued existence. It is simply a tuning-in process that can be accomplished by everyone if they were to allow it. Think of it as a radio tuning into a sound wave. We tune into each other even in our everyday life. The degree to which we tune in differs according to how much we allow ourselves to listen.

By limiting ourselves to the experience of one room in an eight-room house, we never experience the other seven rooms. This is a simple analogy. But this analogy can be used as an example of how we limit our existence as we live our physical life. Since we see only what exists in that one room, we are likely to say that the other seven rooms do not exist, unless we can see them and experience them.

Thus, life after death can be understood by opening our perception and minds to wider possibilities. Only now are people beginning to talk openly about such experiences and journey to the other seven rooms.

It has taken years of learning and experiencing to allow myself to write this book without misconstruing the information through the eyes of my old beliefs. Misconstruing information is one of the mistakes commonly and unwittingly committed by many writers on the subject of death, their misconception being emphasized by their beliefs and especially their fears.

Before any of my major experiences began I was afraid of death. I believed that upon death you lost all consciousness and became nothing, or else met demons, or were to drift endlessly for eternity. This attitude still prevails for many people and the result is that they face death with fear.

From my new vantage point, I see the fear of death as an unnecessarily distressing burden, for death is simply a continuation of your existence. If people clearly understood the process of death and the mechanics of their existence, then they would probably live their present physical life in a more positive and fulfilling fashion. By fearing death and not understanding existence, they do not fully experience or appreciate their time spent in their physical life. They are living in the one room of the eight-room house. Nor do they see that they are on what I like to call a big field trip where they are here to experience and learn the lessons of life and experience the joys of life.

Death no longer has to be that darkened realm feared by the "living." Death is not as terrifying as dramatized in Hollywood movies.

Nor should death create a wall between loved ones who have simply journeyed to a new reality. Think of the added depression and loss when a loved one dies leaving you unsure whether you will ever meet again. But, in reality, it is our lack of understanding that adds to the agony of death. In fact, you will meet again.

My attitude about death began to change with my first communication with a deceased individual. It was my grandmother. She appeared to me about six months after her death. I was eleven. She stood in the doorway of my bedroom and I felt her love. I felt very at peace with her presence that fear was the last thing I could ever feel about the experience. I knew then that life after death was quite probable.

Six years later I had my next experience. A friend named Jim appeared to me a few days after his death.

I first felt his presence in my house. Then one night I awoke to find him standing to the side of my bed. He was looking down at me. I again felt very comfortable with the experience. With his appearance came the beginning of my writing.

My next experience was a very intense personal experience; the death of a friend named Kim. I was eighteen years old. After her death she also returned to visit. In dreams she would talk to me of her experiences in the after-death reality. While awake I would every so often see her appear to me to reassure me of her continued existence. I began keeping a log of all of my dreams and the information that Kim and Jim communicated to me.

Kim, by the way, was reunited with Jim soon after her death. She explained to me that after death you become reunited with friends whom you've always known. She also explained that physical life is a journey that we choose to experience and that some friends choose to stay behind or experience life separately. At the time of death you instantly recall all relationships, not only in the life just ended, but also in previous lives. Death is definitely not a lonely experience.

It is through Jim, Kim, and I that the information contained within this book is passed on to you. But remember that this information is also within your own memory and is not as new to you as you presently believe.

They explained that even though they help in communicating the information, they are actually helping to create a reawakening of knowledge. The knowledge of the after-death existence and all information concerning our eternal existence is actually carried within our memory.

The exercise of tuning into the knowledge is a process that some will not allow themselves to do. Some people are skeptical when they are asked to believe in or even contemplate a new dimension of ideas or a wider area of reality. But they too will die one day and find that they still exist.

I hope this information will help you build a greater understanding of the continuity of life and the non-existence of death.

The existence of life after death is becoming more readily accepted. Someday death will lose its mystery and people will lose their fear of the death transition.

With each new awareness, we become closer to the awareness of God, however you may choose to perceive God and our eternal selves. Life and death are all parts of our ongoing existence. With each new life and each new death we gain insight, growth, and wisdom.

Introduction

When reading *The Death Transition*, read it through once and then read it again if needed, slowly, subject by subject, and picture the process being discussed. Weigh it with your own experiences and consider all possibilities.

If you accept the information easily, let it broaden your understanding of death. If you feel you cannot agree with the book, set it aside and come back to it later.

The explanation of death and the transition of death itself can be written down and it may help the individual to understand his experience in the death transition and the after-death reality. But understand that the experience of each individual upon death may differ somewhat from the experience of someone else. This is because the visions and experiences of an individual are influenced by the needs and the beliefs of that individual and so there are no concrete rules or laws by which the experience or visions of death can be thoroughly anticipated.

Upon death some may see Jesus, some may see Allah, or some may see their Aunt Jane and Uncle Joe. Some may see the famed white light and feel it pulling them towards it. Some may hear voices. Others may hear the wind or quiet. It all stems from the needs and beliefs of the individual upon death. Death is a very personal experience. We see what makes us feel comfortable, see what we expect to see upon death or see what will help us through the transition. Beliefs play a big part in our death experience.

A very religious person will have a higher probability of seeing a religious vision if she believes that she is going to be welcomed by Jesus or Allah or whatever her religious belief may be. On the contrary, a person who feels he is to be punished may momentarily see his own personal hell.

Presently, many people fear and misunderstand death. When finally understood, the transition to death will become an easy movement between two realities and the fear of death will be forgotten.

Death has always been the primary mystery of life only because we feared that which we could not see. The question of death has always been the search for the justification of one's immortality. We have feared the loss of our consciousness and feared damnation because of religious dogma.

What will I find at death? Will I sleep in my grave for eternity or find myself in heaven?

What we must realize is that death is just a transition of reality in which we move from one point of reality or environment to another, much the same as changing our surroundings by moving to a new house or wearing new clothes.

What we must understand is that as individuals we have discarded more bodies than we can now imagine, for we have each lived and died many times before and so death is not such a new experience. This alone should give a clue to our immortality and provide some reassurance.

So the question of death is simply the curiosity and fear of the unknown or shall we say the forgotten. As we begin to accept our eternal existence, we will acquire the ability to understand death and the death reality.

We can now receive hints of this other reality in dreams and experiences that help expand our awareness of its existence. The death of a loved one can bring about communication between you and the deceased in which death and the after-death reality may be shared.

Some religions see death as a positive experience wherein their loved ones travel to the other world. These religions celebrate the death or, rather, the transition of their loved one. Losing a loved one is an emotional experience no matter how we rationalize it. But our view of life and death influences a broad spectrum of who we are and how we deal with these two states of being.

If you picture the after-death reality as a cruel, evil, or empty realm, then you have simply colored it by your fears and beliefs. Try to be receptive to the positive aspects of death and you will begin to understand it is but a transition of form.

Look within yourself as an individual. Forget your beliefs for a few moments and look into your own understanding and weigh the new possibilities of a life that continues on after death. Try to mold this new belief into your present life. If you find that the new idea runs against your beliefs, don't condemn it before you weigh its possibilities.

We must accept the fact that because we exist now in a physical form, in this physical reality, death will someday come to us all. Death is a universal experience that encompasses everything of consciousness. Death carries no prejudice. We will each experience death at our own time no matter what we believe.

As life is supposed to be a positive learning experience so is death and the transition to death.

NOTE

The reference that is made in the text of this book to the terms awake state and sleep state realities are simple references to the way in which physical reality is divided between your waking and sleeping moments.

The awake state is the portion of time in which your main focus is within the physical reality. It is the time in which you are actively going about your physical life. The sleep state is in reference to the time in which your physical body sleeps and you are mentally active in other realities.

Also the reference to your Entity is a reference to your eternal soul that is within you. Think of it as a great computer that has the memory of all of your lives, actions, thoughts, and decisions.

The use of the words "death," "dying," "die," "dead," and "after-death" is for convenience of understanding the ideas presented herein, rather than to perpetuate the fear associated with these terms. It is hoped by the end of this book, you understand there is no death and there are no dead and that the transition between the physical and spirit states is no more than walking from one room into another.

The Death Transition

What Happens Upon Death

The death procedure in itself is easy. At death you simply glide out of your body smooth as a gentle breeze. There is no pain and no struggle. You simply end up outside of your body instead of in it.

In fact, in many cases, the individual will never be aware of the actual moment he leaves his body. He just finds himself outside looking back at his physical body lying in what could be perceived as sleep. Because of this, he may try to re-enter the body not accepting death as the cause of his disassociation. Until the individual understands his new situation or until he accepts his death, he will continue to associate his existence with his physical body.

Upon death some people may see the famed white light and be guided towards it. The light is a visual symbol of your new heightened awareness upon death projected for you to see, for at death you will shed the physical restrictions that bind your thoughts and feelings. Upon death everything is wide open, our feelings, experiences, and responsibilities.

Those who leave their bodies before their time to transition may hear the voice of a guide telling them to return to their earthly lives. The rest will move on and find themselves engulfed in the warm and effervescent feelings of the light.

Some people may see this light as a form of God as they feel and believe that they are moving towards the deity of their beliefs. Strong believers in religion may feel they are moving towards God, Jesus, Allah or other figures that were important to them on the earth plane.

In reality, you will find yourself in surroundings no different than those of physical life. What you see at this moment will depend upon what you believe and what you want to see. You may find yourself at the gates of St. Peter, or you may find yourself in a nice green meadow. You may even find yourself in what appears to be your own home. It all depends on what you expect and what makes you feel the most comfortable and/or what is the most needed to ease your transition.

Pre-Death Guides

Before your death transition occurs you will be greeted by a pre-death guide. This may not occur in all cases but does in the majority of cases. The guide may appear within seconds, minutes, or hours of your departure.

The guide will appear in a form that will best convey trust and security to the individual. The guide may take the form of a religious figure or appear as, or actually be, a friend or relative already in spirit here to meet the individual. The form depends on the needs of the one transitioning.

The pre-death guide will work with the individual in order to emotionally prepare the individual for his death transition. The pre-death guide will most often only be seen by the individual who is dying, though sometimes others may see this presence. The pre-death guide will then help the individual with the death procedure itself, i.e., helping the individual to feel secure enough to leave the body if the individual has fear and if help is needed, and with some post-death adjustment. The most important fact to remember is that the guide is there to help you and for you to listen to and trust in your guide.

In cases of sudden death, such as in an accident or violent act, the guide may or may not be seen before the transition occurs. If the pre-death guide is not seen, the transition will come as a surprise and the individual will not experience the gradual pre-death preparation in which the guide appears in the moments preceding death.

But in cases where the guide is seen while the accident or violent act is occurring he will help direct the individual's focus away from the terror. This will act as a buffer against psychological damage while in the transition state. The buffer is created so that the immediate perception of the after-death reality is not through a confused state of fear and panic. If the victim enters this new reality calm, then he can later go back and experience the accident with a more open view and still benefit from the experience without fear.

In rare cases where the individual may be too involved in the occurring accident or death event to focus otherwise and thus not acknowledge the presence of the guide. Some psychological scars may develop, which the individual must deal with after death. In time, the individual will come to terms with the incident.

Either way, a guide will be there to help in the transition. Death will not be experienced alone. The pre-death guide may also act as your after-death guide in certain cases.

After-Death Guides

You are never alone throughout this whole transition. There will be guides there to help you with your adjustment to death. In some cases, the individual may have two or more guides depending on the circumstances involved. Trust in your guide for he/she will help you in your transition.

After death guides may be friends and relatives. Or they may be people you will not know but who work to help people pass over. Either way you will feel safe and will be safe in your transition.

The After-Death Body

At death, you will feel as though you still exist in a body and in truth you do. For at death, you will have a body, not in a physical sense as you now perceive a body to be, but a body formed by the energy of your entity, energy similar to what creates an aura. But in actuality it is more like the atoms that form matter are electrified to a greater and brighter degree. The energy that is you is vibrating at a higher rate than when you had to sustain the lower vibrational pattern of your physical body.

The spirit body has actually been a part of you throughout your physical life. It has been inside of your physical body all throughout your physical existence. Think of your physical body as a vehicle in which the true you existed until death. At death you will rise from the physical body, your vehicle, and be in this "new" body as you go through the death transition.

This spirit body can be experienced while still in a physical life if the individual experiences what is called an astral travel where the person's spirit body leaves his physical body and travels while the physical body sleeps. People have announced that they have had such real "dreams" where they saw themselves hovering above their sleeping body. The body that hovered in these so-called dreams will be the body you will have upon death.

The body that you will have after-death will look exactly like your physical body because that is how you perceive yourself and what you are used to. In your immediate after-death situation, before the physical body is cremated or buried, you may think you are seeing two identical bodies. You may begin to wonder if the discarded body is not simply an illusion. This won't last long, but it may cause some confusion because you may not at first realize the difference between the old body and your new body, for your image is being projected onto both. But soon the difference will become clear as you begin to understand and accept the mechanics of the transition and you see your physical body wither away in its lifeless state.

The "new" body will be your vehicle in the after-death reality, as your physical body was your vehicle in the physical reality.

The Mourning Process and the Funeral

You will go through many emotions right after death. Emotions will range from disbelief and sorrow to happiness and joy. Again it depends on you and your personal experience in physical life and after transitioning.

Some people may actually mourn their body. They will cling to the body emotionally and may begin to follow it around from the place of death, to the coroner, to the mortician, and finally to the funeral. Such a reaction does not occur in all cases and a guide will be there for you.

You may also experience many emotions from seeing your family in the mourning process and knowing that you will no longer be with them in this life. But you will also know at the same time that you will see them again at a future time. This awareness is intuitive as your understanding becomes clearer.

From the moment you die to the day of your body's funeral, you may spend a large amount of your time focusing on your old body and working to understand your new adjustment. In a majority of cases, there is an extra guest at the funeral who is not seen by other mourners. You will be watching the funeral in a state of awe. You will be hearing all of the things people have to say about you.

All through this process you will have a guide standing with you for guidance and support. The guide will help you throughout. You can hold a conversation with your guide the same way you would with anyone you had known in the physical life.

After the funeral you will begin to release your dependence on the body, since the body by this time is either cremated or buried. Your guide will help you refocus. The guide will help you to move away from the life you just left to the after-death reality.

Missing Body

In cases where the body is not immediately found, as in cases of violent crime or accident, the transitioned individual will be there looking over the body. As stated above the person will be perplexed at seeing his body lying there. But he will be aware that his body is hurt. The individual may try to protect his body and desperately try to revive it. He may even try to go for help in hopes that someone else will be successful in reviving the body. He may go to find relatives and friends to tell them what has happened. He will ask them to try and help.

If he is not successful in communicating and he realizes that no one can hear him or see him, the individual will then return to be by the side of the body. It can be a very emotional time.

The individual will continue to watch over the body, perplexed and mournful until his guides convince him to let go of the emotional hold the individual has on the body. The guides will help refocus the individual and guide him into the after-death reality. Later if the body is found, the individual will have the choice to accompany the body during the forensics, autopsy, funeral, etc. If he does so, the individual will relate to it in a less emotional state depending on how much time has elapsed since their physical death. The individual may choose to also have nothing further to do with body and everything surrounding around it. It will be his choice.

After-Death Environment (Heaven)—Beliefs

What is heaven like? This question has been asked for ages. The answer is that Heaven will be what you think it should be and what you make it. I can hear some readers ask, "what kind of an answer is that?" But the truth is that the Heaven we find is created around our beliefs.

After transitioning some people believe they will see certain set ideas. Christians may believe that they will see angels and the pearly gates with St. Peter there to greet them. Or they may expect to see Jesus standing there to welcome them. Muslims may believe that Allah will greet them and/or that martyrs will receive seventy-two virgins for having sacrificed their life in violence. Jews believe they will spend a year in a purgatory called Gehenna while their souls are being purified and then proceed to heaven.

Those with strong beliefs may actually find that these beliefs have become real. The individual will live in the environment of the beliefs until they adjust to the after-death reality.

Those with a strong belief that they will drift into nothingness after death may actually find themselves in a space of darkness as they sort out their beliefs. But the truth is that even the space of darkness has life. When the individual finally realizes this, they will choose to move out of the darkness and pursue their after-death existence in their new environment. There are many scenarios that are possible. But again it comes back to the individual's beliefs and needs.

I must emphasize again that someone will be there to help you sort everything out. No one will ever be left alone to fend for his or her after-death survival.

After Death Environment (Heaven) —Your Transition Continues

After your initial adjustment, when you start to break free of the visions of your beliefs, your guide will take you to a place where you will feel comfortable and safe. It may look like the home you just left in your physical life. It may be a quiet park with luxurious trees and green grass, if that is what would be best for you. The objective is to take you to a place where you will feel at ease. You may choose to keep some of these as your permanent places of residing while in the after-death environment. Or you may choose other environments that will better suit you as you progress.

From here you will be able to re-adjust comfortably to the death environment. You will be "re-adjusting" for you have transitioned many times from many physical lives. So in truth this is nothing new. You have just forgotten. We have all "died" many times and left behind many bodies.

Your memory of this will return in time. For some people it will return quickly. For others it will return slowly. You will see people from many previous lives. You will be able to see friends and loved ones who passed before you.

Communicating with Loved Ones and Friends

You may choose at this point to communicate with loved ones and friends from your physical life just ended. This may help you to gain perspective on your own situation, but also to reassure your loved ones that you are fine and still exist beyond death.

I had a dream once of my father a few months after his death where he was sitting in a classroom. He was sitting at a school desk reading and writing in a journal. A guide was telling me that he was doing fine and that he was learning. My father then turned to me, smiled and waved at me. He then went back to his journal.

For the individuals who are having a harder time adjusting after death, they may go back to loved ones and friends for help in understanding this dilemma.

If your loved ones are open and receptive, they will be aware of your presence. It will not be the same as when you were living in the same physical reality. They may not necessarily see you but they may actually look your way without realizing that they are doing so.

Don't get frustrated. Try to take it in stride. There is a thin veil between the physical reality and the after-death reality that is difficult to cross. One of the big reasons for this is because your loved one's present belief about life and death causes this divide. When death is more honestly understood, this divide will become less and may actually be able to be penetrated.

If you are reading this book because you have lost someone who has passed over, you will be able to communicate with this individual if you allow yourself to listen. If you allow yourself to be open and observant, you can sense the individual's presence.

You may feel them around you. It may be in the form of feeling their presence in a room to the smelling of the person's perfume or cologne to actually having things move in your house. These are all forms of communication. This works from both sides. Your loved one is trying to communicate with you and your senses are aware of their presence and trying to open up your perceptions. You may actually be able to see your loved one as they appear for a few seconds in your reality. Many people have announced that they have seen a "deceased" loved one standing at the end of their bed.

Communication Through Dreams

You may also begin to communicate to loved ones and friends through dreams. Why dreams? It is because in the sleep state the divide is less between all realities. While your physical loved one is asleep, their consciousness travels to a part of reality where you can meet and talk. While asleep, this communication is viewed as a dream by the ego of the physical loved one. For you it will be no different than if you were holding a conversation while you were alive in the physical world.

When your loved one begins to awake, their consciousness returns to the body. Upon their return, they will bring back with them an interpretation of the communication that their ego will understand. They will see this as a dream that feels extra real, when in reality it was a face-to-face communication.

After Death Environment (Heaven)—Your Transition Continues Farther

After you have comfortably accepted that you have passed over and have gone through some of the first stages of learning about your new environment, you will move farther into the learning stages of your transition.

In this stage you will begin the process of reviewing, evaluating, and learning from the experiences of your life.

This period of time is not always easy for some people for they must look back on their actions in the life just past. In some cases, there is a need to consider lives lived long ago and look at what kind of person you have been as a whole. All of your past lives are available for you to review. Every past life will be important, though some may actually mean less to you emotionally.

This stage is hard for some people because your review is an honest review. In this environment you cannot hide from yourself in denial. You must face the truth. It is the ultimate judgment. People who have been used to looking away and denying their actions in physical life cannot do this in this environment.

You will have your own agenda of what you need to review. In this environment you will be the one choosing your agenda. But as I stated earlier, in this environment honesty is in the forefront. You cannot hide your feelings and emotions as you would in the physical environment. Everyone's goal here is to master who they want to be as a spiritual being as a part of God. It is only in physical life that many hide in denial for they have forgotten who they are as a part of everything, as a part of God.

In this environment you will evolve emotionally and mentally as you become one with yourself, with God, with your whole past and future, and your whole entity. Yes—even your future—for you will be able to see all probabilities available for future lives and you will begin to plan for these if you are choosing to return to physical life.

This can actually now be referred to as the between life environment because after a certain point your past life will no longer be your main focus. It will lose its urgency and you will now be focusing on who you are as a whole being.

As time goes on you will be welcoming other loved ones and friends as they pass over. You may actually help them with their transition and their adjustment.

The between life environment can be a busy time of learning, but it can also have its time of relaxation and quiet reflection. You may choose to take time alone to reflect or you may also choose to relax with loved ones and friends.

If you expect to just die and be left alone to become a recluse it will never happen. You may get your wish momentarily but not forever for you will outgrow the recluse mentality and see its limitations just like those who believed that they would find nothingness after death found momentary darkness. They too outgrew that idea.

The between life environment is a very active environment. It is too active to allow anyone to become stagnant. Your whole entity is also too energetic to allow you to become stagnant and wallow in sorrow and pain and darkness. As you understand the after-death, between life environment, you will no longer resist your existence within it.

The after-death reality is a busy place where people are learning about themselves and their existence. The entity is always learning and always experiencing. It is a positive environment, one where the individual feels the importance of everything she chooses to experience.

This is not meant to be a comparison between realities or to implant the idea that physical reality is a negative reality. For there is beauty to be found in the physical reality as well. This you must search out. Your physical existence is as important as your after-death reality. Both are learning experiences.

Judgment of Past Life

As mentioned above, after transitioning the individual reviews and will judge his past life. He looks at all the things he did and all the things he should have done within that life. The individual's judgment of himself can be harsh depending on the person and their level of perfectionism.

In this new reality all feelings are honest and in the open. The honest evaluation by the individual of all his experiences is the most important factor in his continuous existence. To lie about his achievements and his failures would deprive the individual from a complete understanding of himself and his overall being. In this reality we are aware of the benefit of honesty in guiding and molding our growth.

Killers will realize that they are still alive. Soon they too will realize that their victims also must be alive. Killers have to face their victims and face their actions. This does not mean that the victim will have to face their killer if they choose not to. Guides are able to play the part of the victim if necessary. If a victim does want to face his killer, he is free to do so if he is ready. It is up to the individual.

Killers will find themselves in an intense judgment where they must face every thought, feeling and action from their crime. They will feel the sorrow and pain of their victims. They will not be able to hide from the painful truth of their actions.

Hitler had to face his victims. He had to face the reality of his actions and understand and feel the truth of what his victims felt and all of the repercussions of his actions. All killers will go through the same process including the present day terrorists.

Not everyone is a killer, though, and the review is not that intense. Others will be reviewing their actions as they relate to family members, friends, and everyday situations.

Do they have more to learn about kindness, love, respect, and understanding? Could they have lived their life better? Did they get sidetracked from the original lesson that they were supposed to learn in their life just left?

Planning Your Future Life

The outcome of an individual's past life will influence the choice of his next incarnation and the experiences he will plan. This is one of the main factors forgotten presently in physical reality, that at this moment you are planning the experiences for your next life based upon the experiences of your present life.

The goal of the individual's next life may be to learn the other side of his negative past life choices and to feel what it was like to be on the other side of his past negative actions. He can also choose to continue the positive actions of his last life. The choices are endless, but these are selected based on what is best for the individual.

Whole families may choose to reincarnate together in order to work through issues. They may also choose to come back to simply share in the experience of physical life together. The decision will be based upon the needs of the individuals in the family.

The sadness of war is that the people of a conflict may be caught in a repetitious cycle of changing roles in order to experience the feelings of their enemy. This may occur until the conflict is resolved, especially for an individual who is deeply involved in the conflict or in revenge. This can wreak havoc on generation and after generation, e.g., the conflict in the Middle East.

Many of the problems in physical reality at this moment are caused because people have forgotten their inner knowledge and the benefit of sharing equally the world and environment in which they exist and the advantages and possible growth of sharing in each other's existence. At death, the inner knowledge is revitalized.

As you can see, the individual's past life has a lot of influence over the future experiences of his entity and the choices of his next life. Past life judgment is important and will not always be easy for everyone.

Eternal Doom, Bliss, and the After-Death Reality

Neither eternal doom nor eternal bliss will exist in the after-death environment as you may expect at death.

In the case of eternal bliss, peace will be found upon transitioning, but the after-death reality is not a place of eternal rest. Eternal rest would be too confining and would stifle your experiences, growth, and the creativity of your entity. Eternal rest would turn the individual into a recluse and his awareness would then become ingrown and his experiences would diminish along with his consciousness.

You may also have the desire to find eternal bliss because you are tired of the demands in life and you just want to go to Heaven and have all of your worries and demands disappear. That is not what you will find after transitioning.

The after-death environment is a continued learning experience where you will continue to be an active individual. There is, of course, time for rest as there is time for learning, for everything is balanced.

In the after transitioning environment everyone is equal. There are no class structures, no martyrs, and no divisions as we have created in the physical reality. Everything is based and formed upon individual learning and experiences. Eternal bliss and eternal doom are all created by you.

You may have been taught to believe that bad people will go to a fiery hell where they will suffer for their sins. That will not be the case upon death, but they will have to face all actions from their life during which they hurt others. The truth will be so sharp in this after-death reality that it could feel like a hell for there will be no place to hide from the honest judgment that they will have to face.

PATHWAYS TO MAKING THE TRANSITION

The Death Transition—The Process of Planning

Death is not an instantaneous event that comes unexpectedly as we now believe. Death is actually a gradual process in which you as an individual plan and organize your death probabilities. Some readers at this point may be puzzled and are asking, "what in the world is he talking about? I am not in control of my death."

But in truth you are involved in the planning. Your awake personality is just not aware of it. It all happens behind the scenes. Just as the "deceased" can talk to "living" loved ones in the sleep state, your pre-death planning also happens on other levels of awareness.

Why is it that you are not more aware of your upcoming death? There are multiple reasons. A misunderstanding of death can create an emotional lack of recall. Our beliefs and understanding of life and existence is another. If we believe that death is an end and we will not continue on, then our physical ego will say no to any information that is contrary to what we believe.

Because of our beliefs, much of our everyday planning goes on without us being fully aware of how much of it actually takes place. Some of you may have had dreams where you are mulling over events of the day and making decisions about how you will approach them tomorrow. Then you wake up and take action. You may look upon these moments as simply dreams when in fact these moments are actual work sessions where you are working through something you must face and make a decision about.

Because we block much of the knowledge of our sleep state work sessions, most of the events that happen in our physical life are experienced as major surprises and so is the sudden surprise of death.

Pre-Death Planning

Just as in our everyday life we have work sessions in our sleep state to plan tomorrow; we also have planning sessions in regard to our upcoming death. Pre-death planning work is part of your sleep state planning. We plan and organize the probabilities of our future death events.

In these work sessions you may talk to a relative, a friend or a spiritual guide about your upcoming death probabilities.

In cases where there will be a mass death such as a plane crash or natural disaster, you are aware of the probability that you may share in this catastrophe. You may choose not to participate in the end. The choice is up to you. Our participation in such events helps to send change into the world and is on some level a learning experience.

The behind the scene events of life and death are more active than what we presently perceive.

Timing of Death

The choice by the individual to leave his physical existence and die is usually made when the individual feels he has achieved as much as there is to achieve in this life. He feels the need to move on to a new experience.

There is no set length of stay for an individual. It all depends on what ones desires to experience within physical existence. A child may die because he has found that physical reality was not to his liking. Or an individual may live a very long life in order to experience physical reality in as many ways as possible or to deal with a certain goal, attitude, or fear that one has chosen to try to overcome. There are many different reasons why an individual dies at a given time or in a specific way. Death is a very personal choice.

Sometimes a person's death may end up looking chaotic or prolonged. In many cases, but not all, this is caused because the physical part of the person's awareness and ego are battling with the upcoming death event, i.e., the fear of death, which also involves the clinging to life from the physical perspective of the ego. When the person and his ego finally accept the transition of death, they will allow themselves to pass over.

In the situation of death by murder, accident, etc., death is a little more complex. On some higher level of reality the individual is aware of his probable death and the circumstances that will bring it about. But the physical individual may not be aware because he is blocking it out.

Why would someone want to be murdered or die in an accident? Good question. In the way we presently see life and death, it doesn't make sense that someone would choose that as a way of dying. But in the bigger picture of life and death there is a play being acted out wherein an individual's need to experience a certain reality migrates into the bigger world around them and the beliefs of the world. People dying in the wars and violence of the world, and all circumstances that we would find sorrowful, are participating in this sort of play. People take on parts in these plays and influence the world, globally or locally. While these actions can change the world, these can also change the individuals.

Some people may act out their own play between each other based upon things they feel they each may need to learn and experience. It could be lessons from past lives that need to be resolved. Or it may be that the individual is in a certain state of mind that attracts other participants into his private play. People transmit feelings into the world around them. They may feel it is their time to leave the physical world; they may be in a state of emotional despair and send this feeling out into the world. Their beliefs in what they deserve can also play a part in how they die in a sad death. Whatever our reasons may be, we may never totally understand from a physical frame of mind.

As I mentioned before, it is a complicated and personal experience. As attitudes change and the world changes to a more open and aware emotional environment, these plays will take on a less evasive and dramatic form. Until then, we can watch the news to see these awful plays and wonder why in the world they would choose such actions.

The ultimate answer would be to rid the physical and emotional violence from the individual's world and the physical world as a whole and bring more balance into the ways some people believe they must experience death. Maybe someday, but until then these dramas still filter into the pre-death planning.

In some cases, death may be only a prospect and not actually an event that will be played out. The individual may be leaning towards a death transition but may not be totally ready. Her actions may also be taking her down the road to a death transition. The individual may be looking at his play and wondering if he wants to continue the play as it is or to change it. The death transition looms on one side as a possible action to take and altering the course of his play is another. Again death is a personal choice and can be a complicated decision.

The Transition Begins

When the choice is made to begin the death transition, many changes occur, on both the conscious and sub-conscious levels. The individual slowly begins to alter his primary focus. On a physical level, life may seem very normal, but sub-consciously a psychological change has begun in order to bring the individual closer to his ultimate transition. He may begin to have dreams of his upcoming death or dreams that include symbolism used in order to represent the experience of death and/or the mechanics of the death reality. He could have dreams of packing a suitcase to go on a trip. He may have dreams where he is visiting family and saying good-bye. Or he may be having dreams where he is re-living past events more than usual. What a person sees depends on how the ego interprets the message to the physical person. He may even choose to see nothing.

On a physical level, the person may begin to outwardly express the sub-conscious events in his actions. The individual may also get sentimental about his life memories and experiences. He may find a renewed interest in religion as he comes closer to his transition, or due to the fear of death. Or he may feel an urgent need to write a will or finish uncompleted projects without actually realizing the significance of his actions. These are just possible examples. Again it comes down to the individual and how he wants to experience it.

In the sleep state, the main organizing continues. The individual is planning the circumstances, the mode, and the timing of his death. An individual's death is not a total surprise to family and friends. For at some point in their subconscious, the family is aware of the individual's choice to leave physical existence and the meaning beneath the drama of his death. But again, in the awake state they may deny this subconscious information and continue to see the event as a total surprise.

In dreams, family members may see the individual getting ready to leave on a trip. They may experience the good-bye dream. Death is an interactive experience shared by all that will be affected. The contents of the dream will differ for each individual. Of course, some may never have these dreams.

The way that the individual handles this transition process will start to become visible in the mannerisms and actions of the individual, even if the individual is not aware of the significance.

Senility

Our fears and beliefs can also create such pre-death trauma as senility. In this case the fear of death causes the awake state personality to cling to physical reality out of fear of the unknown and fear of letting the physical body go. The awake state personality is afraid that without the physical body it will become non-existent.

Because of the fear of death, the awake state personality tests the after-death reality by degree until it is satisfied that death is not to be feared. The awake state personality then proceeds with its complete death transition.

While in the state of senility, the outward physical appearance is one of mental impairment because the main consciousness of the individual is focused in the after-death reality. This leaves a smaller portion of consciousness in physical reality in order to keep the body functioning and to keep some hold on physical reality.

The degree of consciousness that the individual transfers to the after-death reality depends on the individual. In the beginning, very little consciousness is transferred and this is why senility can overcome an individual gradually. As the individual becomes more at ease with the after-death reality, the senility deepens, followed by death.

The individual freely moves between the two realities, testing and exploring death. When the individual moves between the state of senility and physical mental alertness, his main consciousness is simply moving from the physical reality to the after-death reality and back, much the same as moving between the sleep state to the awake state as we do every time we awake from sleep.

When a disease is diagnosed as the cause for senility, the disease is still the creation of the individual in his desire to lower his physical experience. The disease is just another added experience as well as a deterrent to his continued physical existence.

Coma

Coma is similar to senility. The difference is that senility is caused by a fear of death, where coma is caused by mental and/or physical shock due to illness or accident.

While in the state of coma, the individual will use this time to bring his physical existence into perspective and to choose his future primary direction. The individual will either coordinate the healing of the physical body or find the body not in his future plans and leave it entirely and then merge into the after death reality, causing physical death.

The state of coma may also be used as a time of rest from mental and psychological shock. The individual has been thrown into a state of such intense confusion that by leaving physical reality he regains a perspective on his life. He may then choose to return to physical reality or he may not. The possibility of the individual remembering his coma state reality upon his return depends solely on the individual and the acceptance of the awake state personality.

In cases where the body continues to function and the individual has not returned it to a full state of physical activeness, it is the body which continues to live while the main consciousness of the individual exists in the after-death reality.

The people who know the individual in his physical form will continue to view him in a total physical aspect. They will consider the body to be the complete individual without realizing that they are actually looking at an empty or semi-empty vehicle and that the individual is active elsewhere. If the family can begin to see his coma from the new perspective they can encourage his work by talking to the individual for he will be able to hear the conversation. But the individual still has the final say as to whether or not he will return to the physical reality.

In circumstances where life-sustaining machinery is used, an artificial illusion is created of life that is actually just the prolonging of the empty physical body.

It must be realized that the body is separate from the individual, the soul, and that no amount of resuscitation will bring back the individual before he chooses to return, if at all.

Partial Death Experience

In most cases when it is not the right time for the individual to die, there will not be a pre-death guide to meet him on the beginning part of the transition. This is simply because no pre-death planning has taken place. In most cases, someone will speak to the individual on the other side and they will re-emphasize the importance that the individual return to the physical reality.

On his return, he may or may not remember the after-death experience simply because it may go against his beliefs regarding death and the mechanics of physical reality. However, if the individual does remember his near-death experience, it will most often change his belief on life after death and his attitude towards physical life in general including his overall existence.

In some ways, the individuals who experience the after-death environment in a partial death experience can act as messengers for the after-death reality. They may not realize the importance of their experiences in influencing a change in society's belief and understanding of death. But by speaking out on their personal experiences, they allow others to weigh the possibilities of life after death.

Different experiences such as a partial death experience, dreams, astral projection, and awake state premonitions can give the individual a chance to touch the after-death reality. It is up to the individual to pursue and develop his understanding of life and death.

Suicide

When an individual commits suicide, he does not instantly go to hell or to an eternal punishment. Instead the experience that he will discover will be based upon his belief. If he believes that he must be punished for his actions, he may have an experience based upon that belief momentarily. But that will not last. An after-death guide will let the individual know that punishment is not merited and not required.

The individual will be surprised to still have consciousness if they expected to annihilate their consciousness by committing suicide. They will soon learn that consciousness cannot be destroyed. It is a part of their eternal essence.

They will also be surprised by the heightened awareness of their emotions and the awareness of the emotions of the friends and loved ones they left behind.

Some individuals may have regrets and become frustrated and sorry that they chose suicide. But of course they will soon need to come to the understanding that they cannot undo their action.

After death the individual will have to face their actions with total honesty and come to terms with their successes and their failures. They will have put to an end the life they had planned and will have to repeat the lessons that were not learned. They will also have to deal honestly with the effect that they had on others due to the choices that they made both in life and in their mode of death. Suicide is not the end of responsibility or of an individual's existence. They may regret the choice they made due to their momentary desperation. They may also be disappointed to find that they still exist.

It must be remembered that as in a planned death, an after-death guide will be there for the individual to help them through their transition following a suicide.

The Tunnel and the Bright Light

The common vision of rising through a tunnel towards a very bright light is a symbolic way to show the rise in consciousness experienced upon death. The light is a combination of knowledge and energy. The tunnel is not a fixed structure that is discovered by all who die, but rather a mental illusion, a conveyance of symbolism to those who will relate to its existence.

The Individual Creates His/Her Experiences

The experience of death depends solely on the individual, for some adjust quickly and others more slowly. It all depends again on the individual's beliefs. But eventually everyone adjusts to the after-death environment.

Death is part of the continuous cycle of your existence. You live, you die, and you live again. But in truth, you just discard your physical body and move on, focused in a different reality. Never dying, always living.

The experience of death, as in life is the experience you create.

If you are calm and inquisitive about your new situation and receptive to the answers your guide will give you, then your adjustment will be fast and easy. But there are those who will fight, panic, and refuse to accept any existence other than physical existence or a set belief on death. They will refuse to accept or even believe that they have died. Even though they exist after death, they will refuse to accept life after death as a possibility.

In some cases, the individual has no idea that he has any control over his environment or existence and refuses to take responsibility for the after-death environment that he is creating.

It is because of this refusal at death that the individual must then relearn the truth behind his own existence, his influence over his environment, and his freedom to create. The human race has lost such an understanding and so, upon death, the individual must re-adjust to freedom on a higher personal level.

"In this reality we are at peace with our creativity and our existence. We experience our existence on a higher level of perception. For in this environment, our creativity is obvious since our thoughts create our immediate environment".

"In the physical environment, the perception of your creativity is less obvious due to your present concept of reality, your beliefs and the limits they create. Your belief in time as a domineering force also is a major limit which you have placed on your existence and your experiences".

"Since our thoughts are instantaneous and the mere thought of an object or landscape will make it appear, you may think the after death reality would be very disorganized and crowded. But there is coordination in all visual projections. For we can share with each other to create a combined visual environment in which we all agree. Or if we choose, we can create an environment of momentary privacy".

"One moment we could be sitting in a crowd of people, and the next moment we could choose to sit alone. It all reverts back to our thoughts and our freedom of choice. Reality here is free from all restraint. The crowd of people still exists, but we have simply looked away from their idea of reality to a different one of our own for the time being".

"Reality is not stacked one on top of another. Reality is more of a blending together. In the room you are in at this moment, there are other realities also sharing the same space. But you cannot see them as they cannot always see you. We are each projecting different ideas of environments and seeing only our own creations. If we choose to, we can see each other. Sometimes you can catch a glimpse of a different reality, but most often you simply ignore it or see it as an illusive flash".

Visions Upon Death

Since within the after-death reality our beliefs form our environment, our strongest inner thoughts will become reality. For those of strong religious conviction their visions may be influenced by their religious beliefs. Christians may meet Jesus, Buddhists may meet Buddha,

Muslims may meet Allah, and so on depending on the religion.

For those without such beliefs, the religious dramas may be totally bypassed and other visions will take precedence depending on the needs of the individual. Some may find themselves in a great landscape of beauty and peace. Others may find themselves walking towards the home where they were born with a loved one waiting at the door with open arms ready to embrace them.

These visions may, in physical terms, be classified as fantasies or hallucinations. But within this reality the visions are legitimate. They are simply outward expressions of the inner need of the individual manifested into reality.

Within these visions you will be able to smell, taste, and feel all that you now can sense within physical reality. But in the after-death reality, your senses will be magnified to a brilliant proportion beyond the senses of physical reality. The blue of the sky may be the bluest you have ever witnessed or the air the freshest. There are no definite visions that will be encountered by all upon death since all visions are actually the personal expression of the individual.

Death is simply the changing of your perception from one reality to another. There is no mysterious, evil force awaiting your arrival upon transitioning and this transition is not an end to consciousness nor is it an eternal sleep. Nor are there rewards of martyrdom or golden castles other than what you may temporarily perceive.

No Boundaries

There is no limit to the amount of knowledge you can receive or the experiences you can experience. In the after-death reality, you will find freedom beyond any freedom you could now imagine in physical existence. There are no boundaries in the after death reality other than the boundaries you create. The same applies to physical reality. Psychological boundaries are your limitations in the physical reality.

Importance of Your Physical Life

It must be emphasized that the physical life that you experience now is very important. There are lessons to be learned that only you can learn in a physical reality.

The freedom of the after-death reality is mentioned in this book, but it is not meant as an invitation to leave your present physical life behind. You must learn the lessons that you have come to learn in the physical life. If you leave early then you will most likely choose to return to finish the lesson in a next life.

Use the information written in this book as knowledge of your immortality. You are a person of great importance and learning. Use this information as a tool to adjust your beliefs and understanding of your limitless existence.

COMMUNICATING WITH LOVED ONES IN SPIRIT

Communications with the Deceased

Communication in all forms consists of a tuning in process. Be it with a dial of a radio or the focusing your undivided attention in a conversation with a friend.

Communications with a deceased friend or relative also entails a tuning in process. But when such communication does occur, it is often not recognized for its true source. People may put this communication into a category such as a fantasized dream or a nightmare, not accepting it as a legitimate communication.

Our beliefs influence how we view these messages and they can interfere with our ability to receive. For if your beliefs are strong that life after death does not exist, or you are afraid of such experiences, then you may block your awake state from receiving communication from other realities. For those who have no set belief either way, the chance for communication is greater. The best chance for open communication will occur for those who believe life after death is a possibility.

It is the process of clearing this path of communication that will lead to an open channel between you and the deceased.

Remember that realities are divided only by a fine line of perception. It is our focus that creates the division between different realities. By letting go of our strict idea of limits within our existence, we will allow our senses to travel beyond this fine line.

It is a change of attitude and acceptance that will reunite loved ones beyond death. With such a new awareness, you will also be able to gain insight into your own soul, its complexity, and your own true existence.

In the first few weeks or months after the death of a loved one, the communication will most often be more active. This is because the deceased is still in an early transition stage and still focusing on his physical family and friends. He is also still overwhelmed by his new environment and still clings to a degree to his image in physical life.

As he becomes more accustomed to the after-death reality, his focus will turn towards his guides and his learning. This is not meant to suggest that he is abandoning his family and friends in physical reality, but rather that he needs to direct his focus towards his adjustment and education. Communication will still continue if all parties desire it, but it may be less frequent than before.

You must also realize that since you still exist in the physical reality, you must therefore continue with your everyday existence. Your dependence on the deceased must be adjusted to fit the new situation. In fact, the deceased may express this point to you in a communication if he feels that you are overemphasizing your dependence on him and thus ignoring the importance of your own existence and the goals you must accomplish. In this way the deceased is helping the "living" to come to terms with the new situation.

The love for loved ones in the physical reality will still continue and there will always be a close bond between the two if it is allowed to continue. It is usually the "living" who deny the continuance of this love either out of guilt or a feeling of not being loved by the deceased because of the belief that the deceased deserted them by dying.

It is usually the deceased who will first try to change this misconception, but will, in many cases, be denied communication by your reluctance to remain open to it. In any case it is best to resolve and come to terms with all problems for both parties. Death is not a punishment and death is not an end to a relationship.

If you feel anger or resentment at the death of a loved one, or feel betrayed by his leaving, you must remember that the choice made by the individual to leave physical existence was a long thought out decision and was in the best interest of the deceased, even if the "living" can't accept it.

Just remember that your relationship with the deceased will always exist and that someday you will meet again. But for now communication can continue between the physical and death realities. Be open to its opportunities.

First Communication—The Presence

The first communication with a deceased friend or relative will most often consist of a feeling of the individual's presence next to you. This may occur within the first or second day of the individual's transition.

Try to accept his presence as legitimate. Try to focus on the feelings you are experiencing and any feeling that he is trying to convey to you. Listen and be open.

Remember that the individual is still as real as you are. The only difference is that he no longer has a body that you can see. But he still feels emotion and thought and is probably very amazed and maybe a little confused by his new situation.

Don't worry that your imagination might be getting the best of you. The intensity of his presence will be strong enough to enable you to discern the difference between an actual communication and your imagination. The individual will feel as real as if he was still alive in a physical sense.

This type of experience happens every day. The people who have such experiences either allow themselves to witness it or else they brush it off as a coincidental oddity with no legitimate substance. In fact, what they are actually doing is tuning out their loved ones and shutting a door. To be able to communicate with your loved one in spirit, you must open up the door and allow him his continued existence. There is no need for a wall to be built between family and friends.

If you are open to your surroundings and allow such a communication, then you will sense their presence and they will re-confirm their love for you.

Second Communication—The Dream

The second communication is usually in the form of a dream. It may occur within the first three weeks from the individual's death and usually not until after the funeral. Of course it can happen at any time since all communication is of a personal preference.

The reason for the occurrence after the funeral is that in most cases the individual is so involved with his adjustment and the activity surrounding the body, that little time is spent focusing anywhere else. After the funeral the old body is gone and his focus is usually released. He will then proceed with his adjustment, in most cases, want to communicate to his "living" friends and family of his continued existence.

The dreams will usually occur naturally without any need for preparation on your part. They will just occur as any other dream.

The dream will feel very legitimate and real. It will feel as if you were talking face to face with the individual and he was still physically alive. If the two of you touch each other within the dream, it will feel as though he was still in a physical body.

In truth, the two of you actually did touch. Not with your physical body, but with your sleep state body. For your sleep state body is as real in that reality as your physical body is in the physical reality. The sleep state body is actually the same body as your after-death body mentioned earlier.

Don't be alarmed by such realism, for it is still your loved one that you are touching. There is no need to be afraid.

When you awake from the dream, immediately before getting out of bed write down the dream and everything that was said in detail. Start a journal. Write down the date of the dream and the time you awoke. This journal will act as a tool to develop your awareness and your communicating abilities.

In case you have trouble in communicating or remembering your dreams, here are a few suggestions that may help.

If the problem is remembering the dream, then try to program yourself before you go to sleep. As you fall asleep, tell yourself over and over again to remember the dream and try picturing yourself succeeding. You are simply sending a message to your awake state personality.

If you awake the next morning or after the dream and feel as though you have a shadowy remembrance of a dream, take some time to dig for the dream and pull it to the surface of your awake state. If you remember just one detail of the dream sometimes the rest of the dream will follow. Even if you remember only a small detail write it down.

It is best if you put yourself in a frame of mind that is open and receptive. If you really do not believe in life after death as a possibility and consider communicating with the deceased as unrealistic, then you may create your own defeat. But if you are open minded, then with practice you may succeed.

As you begin to fall asleep, think of the deceased and picture the two of you talking. While doing this, try to catch the essence of the individual and feel his personality. Do not picture the individual as the physical dead corpse or as a ghost, for that may cause your fear of death to block the communication. Picture the individual as he was when he was physically alive. Also try to picture what he is doing in his new environment.

Do all of these preparations very calmly and never force it. By forcing it you may end up trying too hard and become frustrated and build yet another wall.

Be relaxed about your experiment and let yourself glide into sleep. Experience whatever occurs and write it down in your journal. If no communication occurs, don't get disappointed. Simply try it another night.

If you end up not communicating with your deceased loved ones, you may end up receiving communication from someone who knows the individual in the after-death reality. This person may update you on your loved one and his progress. Just take it as it comes and be patient. This mode of communicating with spirit may not be right for everyone and so it may not work for everyone. Or it may not be the right time.

Incidentally, the longer the individual has been deceased, the harder it may be to communicate, since the individual will have changed his focus more towards his new reality. It is best if the communication begins soon after the death of the individual. You will see the individual again at a later date.

Third Communication—The Physical Appearance

The third communication is a little less frequent in its occurrence. An appearance by the individual is usually used as a very special reassurance to his loved ones of his continued existence and continued caring, or as a deliverance of a message. If an appearance does not occur, it does not mean the individual doesn't care, for appearances are not always necessary.

The form which the individual will take in an appearance will not be physical in the terms by which you view your body. The difference in an appearance is that the individual is creating this body only momentarily. You are actually an active participant in its creation, for the individual is sending to the physical reality a strong portion of his essence. You hold a subconscious impression of what you consider to be the outside appearance of the individual. Thus, you help to create this outside appearance from this impression as well as with the help of the individual's suggestion. He may look younger, healthier. Don't be alarmed if the appearance consists of only half the body, because you both have agreed that the legs and feet may not be an important part of the appearance.

The appearance is similar to the first communication where you feel only the presence. The appearance is just a more powerful expression by the individual. The different degree in the clarity of the manifestation depends on how much you will allow yourself to perceive.

The appearance of the individual will usually occur when you least expect it because there will be less resistance on your part. Of course on some level of your subconscious you were aware of its pending emergence.

Never be afraid of the individual if he does make an appearance, for it is a gesture of love and caring. There will be no evil spirits manifesting as in the horror movies. They do not exist other than when created out of your fears.

The three forms of communication just mentioned may not always occur in that order or may not even occur at all in some cases. It is up to the individuals involved. I just hope that from this understanding, loved ones will begin to build an open channel of communication and love beyond physical death.

I also hope that *The Death Transition* will help those who are still "living" in the physical realm to understand better what their deceased family and friends are now experiencing and view their transition as a new beginning. I also hope this will help to ease the fear of death and make everyone's transition an easy and peaceful journey.

REMINDERS

The Appearance of the Pre-Death Guide

Your guide will appear within seconds, minutes, or hours of your death and will be seen by only you. He/she will appear as real to you as if he/she existed in a physical body.

Remember that the guide may appear as anything from a family member to a religious figure. The identity will depend solely on you and the identity to which you will best relate. Your guide may in fact be an actual relative here to help. In either case, trust in your guide and listen to what he/she has to say. For your guide will help you to proceed with the death transition. Your physical death will follow at the moment you release your body.

The guide may appear many times just prior to your physical death. Don't be alarmed if your guide disappears for he/she will re-appear in time to guide you through your transition. Your guide plays a very important role in your adjustment to the after-death reality. Trust in your guide's advice.

Death

When you find yourself outside of your body, stay calm and don't panic. Slowly look around and observe your surroundings.

Don't come to any sudden conclusions about your new situation. If you are positive that you have died and you accept it, experience it slowly and keep a positive attitude about it. If you are not sure of your situation, take a closer look at your surroundings and your present experiences.

If you try and re-enter your body and find that you can't, continue to stay calm. Try to accept the fact that you can't re-enter your body simply because you have chosen to discard it.

If there are other individuals near you, but who cannot hear or see you, this is another sign of death. Continue to stay calm. This does not mean you are non-existent, for if you can see these other individuals, then your consciousness is obviously still intact. You are just in a different reality from theirs.

If you do panic then simply close your eyes and try to relax. Look around for your guide if he or she is not in sight or you've lost your guide due to your confusion. Know that your guide has never left. Your guide will be the person who can see you, speak to you, and hear you. The guide will help you with any questions you may have. Trust in your guide, for your guide is there to help you. Remember that some individuals may have two or more guides.

If you feel you must go visiting or follow your body, do so if it will help you with your adjustment. Take a guide along with you (your guide will go anyway) and will help you to understand and deal with any emotions or situations that will arise.

You may go to your own funeral. You will be the one extra guest that the mourners don't see. Watching your own funeral can be an emotional experience. It can also be an awe evoking one. When it is over then it will be time to move on.

After you have mastered this ability, you will be able to travel anywhere you want to go. Remember that you have done all of this many times before and that you are not alone after death.

After you have adjusted to your new situation and accepted your death, it will be time to move further into your after-death existence. At this point you will meet a new guide who will take over for the pre-death guide who dealt with the immediate after-death situation. This new guide will be your teacher for the rest of the after-death adjustment. He/she will teach you all there is to learn about your existence. Remember that in some cases the pre-death guide may also be your after-death guide in which case no change will occur.

At this point you will start to meet many old friends whom you have visited in your dream communications and have known in past lives. Enjoy your ongoing existence and all your friends. You have crossed the death transition again.

Out of everything that was previously mentioned, there are a few important things to remember, even if you forget the rest. Stay calm, listen, and trust your guide or guides.

You may think a book would be useless after death since "you can't take it with you," physically. But remember, that as you read this book, your mind is storing the knowledge. In the after-death state, you can have this book appear, since your thoughts create reality, both in the physical and the after death realities.

Existence on the spiritual plane is a positive, active, and growing experience as is physical existence. You will be as alive after transitioning as you always have been and as you always will be for eternity. Death is a transition, not an ending.

QUESTIONS

If you have questions you may e-mail them to
Deathtransition@yahoo.com or visit www.deathtransition.com

CONVERSATION

If you would like to join the conversation follow me on **Twitter**

at https://twitter.com/deathtransition

THANKS

Thanks to everyone who has helped to promote my book and get

the word out that we still exist after death.

SELECTED READING

Alexander III M.D., Eben, Proof of Heaven, Simon & Schuster, 2012

McConnell, Kathleen, Don't Call Then Ghosts – The Spirit Children of Fontaine Manse – A True Story Llewellyn Publications 2004

Moorjani, Anita, Dying To Be Me, Hay House, Inc. 2012

Roberts, Jane, *Seth Speaks*, Amber-Allen Publishing and New World Library, 1994

23579949R00051

Printed in Great Britain
by Amazon